ILLINOIS

EXPLORE THE UNITED STATES

Julie Murray

Big Buddy BOOKS
Explore the United States

VISIT US AT
www.abdopublishing.com

Published by ABDO Publishing Company, PO Box 398166, Minneapolis, MN 55439.

Printed in the United States of America, North Mankato, Minnesota.
032012
092012

♻ PRINTED ON RECYCLED PAPER

Coordinating Series Editor: Rochelle Baltzer
Editor: Sarah Tieck
Contributing Editors: Megan M. Gunderson, BreAnn Rumsch, Marcia Zappa
Graphic Design: Adam Craven
Cover Photograph: *Shutterstock*: John Lindsay-Smith.
Interior Photographs/Illustrations: *Alamy*: National Geographic Image Collection (p. 13); *AP Photo*: AP Photo (p. 23), Charles Rex Arbogast (p. 21), Seth Perlman (p. 27), Barry Thumma (p. 25); *Getty Images*: Willard Clay/Oxford Scientific (p. 17), Jack Rosen/Photo Researchers (p. 30); *iStockphoto*: iStockphoto.com/filo (p. 30), iStockphoto.com/iStockphoto.com/ghornephoto (pp. 11, 23), iStockphoto.com/groveb (p. 19), iStockphoto.com/Kubrak78 (p. 27), iStockphoto.com/nazdravie (p. 27), iStockphoto.com/Solange_Z (p. 26), iStockphoto.com/uschools (p. 19); *Shutterstock*: blewisphotography (p. 9), S.Borisov (p. 9), Steve Byland (p. 30), Philip Lange (p. 30), Eugene Moerman (p. 5), Henryk Sadura (pp. 11, 26), Yaro (p. 29).

All population figures taken from the 2010 US census.

Library of Congress Cataloging-in-Publication Data

Murray, Julie, 1969-
 Illinois / Julie Murray.
   p. cm. -- (Explore the United States)
 ISBN 978-1-61783-351-9
 1. Illinois--Juvenile literature. I. Title.
 F541.3.M875 2013
 977.3--dc23
                    2012004278

ILLINOIS

★★★★★★★★★★★★★★★★★★★★★★★★★★★★★★★★★★★★

Contents

One Nation

   The United States is a **diverse** country. It has farmland, cities, coasts, and mountains. Its people come from many different backgrounds. And, its history covers more than 200 years.

   Today the country includes 50 states. Illinois is one of these states. Let's learn more about Illinois and its story!

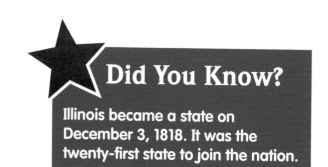

Did You Know?

Illinois became a state on December 3, 1818. It was the twenty-first state to join the nation.

Chicago is a major city in Illinois. It is known for its tall buildings. The Willis Tower is one of the world's tallest buildings!

ILLINOIS UP CLOSE

The United States has four main **regions**. Illinois is in the Midwest.

Illinois shares borders with five other states. Iowa and Missouri are west. Wisconsin is north, Indiana is east, and Kentucky is southeast. Lake Michigan is northeast.

Illinois has a total area of 57,916 square miles (150,002 sq km). It is the fifth-largest state in population. More than 12.8 million people live there.

REGIONS OF THE UNITED STATES

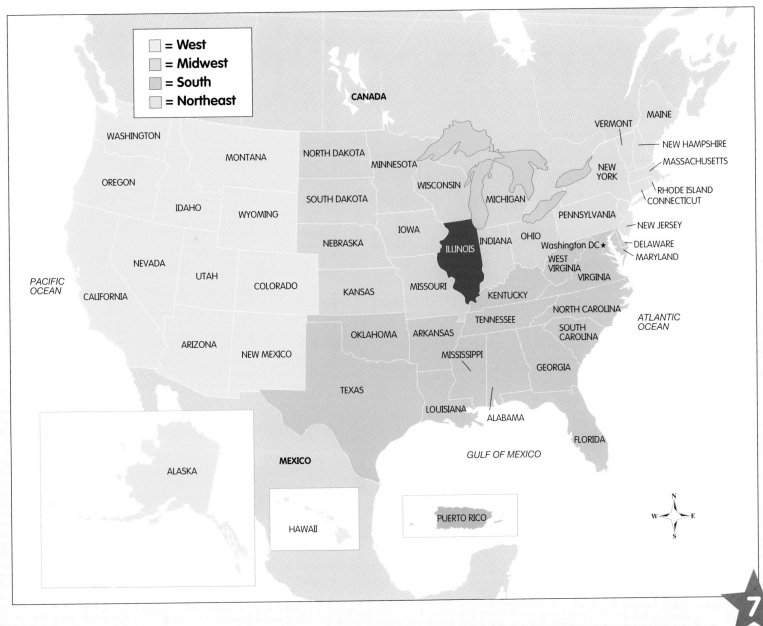

= West
= Midwest
= South
= Northeast

CANADA

WASHINGTON
OREGON
MONTANA
IDAHO
WYOMING
NORTH DAKOTA
MINNESOTA
SOUTH DAKOTA
WISCONSIN
MICHIGAN
VERMONT
MAINE
NEW HAMPSHIRE
MASSACHUSETTS
NEW YORK
RHODE ISLAND
CONNECTICUT
PENNSYLVANIA
NEW JERSEY
NEVADA
UTAH
COLORADO
NEBRASKA
IOWA
ILLINOIS
INDIANA
OHIO
Washington DC ★
DELAWARE
MARYLAND
WEST VIRGINIA
VIRGINIA
PACIFIC OCEAN
CALIFORNIA
ARIZONA
NEW MEXICO
KANSAS
MISSOURI
KENTUCKY
TENNESSEE
NORTH CAROLINA
SOUTH CAROLINA
ATLANTIC OCEAN
OKLAHOMA
ARKANSAS
TEXAS
MISSISSIPPI
GEORGIA
LOUISIANA
ALABAMA
FLORIDA
GULF OF MEXICO
ALASKA
MEXICO
HAWAII
PUERTO RICO

N
W E
S

IMPORTANT CITIES

Chicago is the largest city in Illinois. It is also the third-largest city in the United States! Its population is 2,695,598. Chicago is located on Lake Michigan. It is known as "the Windy City."

Aurora is the state's second-largest city. It is home to 197,899 people. Aurora is called "the City of Lights." It was one of the first US cities to use electric streetlights.

Did You Know?

Lake Michigan is one of the five Great Lakes.

ILLINOIS

Rockford●
Aurora● ●Chicago

★Springfield

N
W E
S

Cloud Gate is a famous piece of public art in downtown Chicago. Most people simply call it "the Bean."

Boating on Chicago's waterways is a popular activity.

9

Rockford is the third-largest city in Illinois. It has 152,871 people. Rockford is known as "the Forest City" because of its many parks and trees.

Springfield is the state's **capital**. This city is known for its history. President Abraham Lincoln lived there for many years.

The Rock River flows through Rockford.

Since Illinois became a state, it has had six capitol buildings. The current capitol building (*left*) was completed in 1888.

11

ILLINOIS IN HISTORY

The history of Illinois includes Native Americans and settlers. Around AD 700, Native Americans started a community near present-day Cahokia. This became the largest Native American community north of Mexico. By 1100, up to 20,000 people lived there!

French explorers first visited Illinois in 1673. Later, French settlements were built there. In 1763, England took control of the area. Illinois became a state in 1818.

Cahokia Mounds is a World Heritage Site. This means it will be protected because it is important to world history.

Timeline

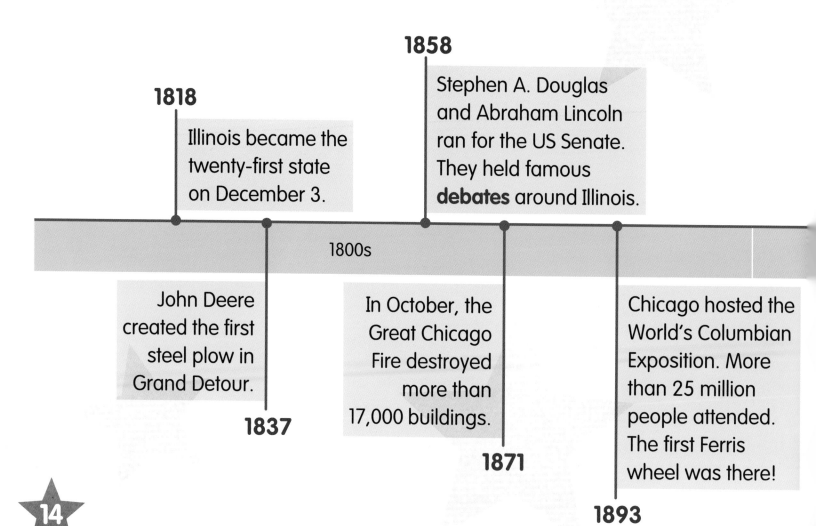

1818

Illinois became the twenty-first state on December 3.

1858

Stephen A. Douglas and Abraham Lincoln ran for the US Senate. They held famous **debates** around Illinois.

1800s

John Deere created the first steel plow in Grand Detour.

1837

In October, the Great Chicago Fire destroyed more than 17,000 buildings.

1871

Chicago hosted the World's Columbian Exposition. More than 25 million people attended. The first Ferris wheel was there!

1893

1950

Gwendolyn Brooks of Chicago became the first African-American poet to win a Pulitzer Prize. It was for a book of poems called *Annie Allen*.

2011

Longest-serving Chicago mayor Richard M. Daley decided not to run for office again. Rahm Emanuel became Chicago's mayor.

1900s

2000s

The National Association for the Advancement of Colored People (NAACP) was formed after fights over race in Illinois broke out.

Many parts of Illinois were harmed when the Mississippi River flooded.

US senator Barack Obama of Illinois became the forty-fourth president. He was the first African American to be US president!

1909

1993

2009

ACROSS THE LAND

Illinois has farms, forests, and flat, grassy land. It has many important bodies of water. One major waterway is the Mississippi River. Lake Michigan is another. It is the only Great Lake entirely in the United States.

Many types of animals make their homes in Illinois. These include white-tailed deer, foxes, and walleye.

Did You Know?

The weather in Illinois changes with the seasons. The average July temperature is 76°F (24°C). In January, it is 26°F (-3°C).

The Mississippi River is the country's largest river.
It forms the entire western border of Illinois.

Earning a Living

Illinois has many important businesses. One is farming. The state's major crops are corn and soybeans.

Other businesses include shipping, finance, **media**, and manufacturing. The state makes food, electronics, and rubber products.

Transportation is another major business in Illinois. Chicago is a transportation center for the whole country.

O'Hare International (*right*) and Midway International are the state's major airports.

Chicago's railroads handle more freight than any other part of the country.

19

SPORTS PAGE

Many people think of sports when they think of Illinois. The state is home to football, baseball, basketball, hockey, and soccer teams.

Many fans follow the Chicago Bears football team and the Chicago Bulls basketball team. Chicago also has two baseball teams! They are the Cubs and the White Sox.

Chicago Bears fans are proud supporters of their team!

21

HOMETOWN HEROES

Many famous people have lived in Illinois. Abraham Lincoln was born in Kentucky in 1809. But, he lived in Springfield from 1837 to 1861. There, he got married, started a family, and began government work.

Lincoln became the US president on March 4, 1861. He worked hard to keep the country together during the **American Civil War**. He is also famous for helping to end **slavery**.

Visitors to Springfield can see a
home where Lincoln once lived.

Lincoln was the sixteenth US president.

Ronald Reagan was born in Tampico in 1911. He became famous for his work in acting and **politics**.

Reagan was an actor in Hollywood from the late 1930s to the 1950s. He became governor of California in 1967. From 1981 to 1989 he served as US president. He worked to settle problems between the United States and the Soviet Union.

Reagan was the fortieth US president.

Tour Book

Do you want to go to Illinois? If you visit the state, here are some places to go and things to do!

★ Explore

Visit a beach on Lake Michigan. You could take a boat ride, build a sand castle, or have a picnic.

★ Remember

Spend the day in Galena. This city is near the Mississippi River and has many old buildings. You can even visit the home of past US president Ulysses S. Grant.

★ Cheer

Watch a Chicago Cubs baseball game at Wrigley Field!

★ Discover

The Abraham Lincoln Presidential Library and Museum is in Springfield. It has life-size figures of Lincoln and his family!

★ Ride

Chicago has a famous train system known as the "L." It got this name because it is elevated, or above the ground.

A GREAT STATE

The story of Illinois is important to the United States. The people and places that make up this state offer something special to the country. Together with all the states, Illinois helps make the United States great.

The Chicago River is one of many important waterways in Illinois.

Fast Facts

Date of Statehood:
December 3, 1818

Population (rank):
12,830,632
(5th most-populated state)

Total Area (rank):
57,916 square miles
(25th largest state)

Motto:
"State Sovereignty, National Union"

Nickname:
Prairie State,
Land of Lincoln

State Capital:
Springfield

Flag:

Flower: Violet

Postal Abbreviation:
IL

Tree: White Oak

Bird: Northern Cardinal

Important Words

American Civil War the war between the Northern and Southern states from 1861 to 1865.
capital a city where government leaders meet.
debate a planned discussion or argument about a question or topic, often held in public.
diverse made up of things that are different from each other.
media ways of sharing information, especially with large groups of people. Radio, television, newspapers, and magazines are examples of media.
politics the art or science of government.
region a large part of a country that is different from other parts.
slavery the practice of owning people as slaves. A slave is a person who is bought and sold as property.
transportation the act of moving people or things from one place to another.

Web Sites

To learn more about Illinois, visit ABDO Publishing Company online. Web sites about Illinois are featured on our Book Links page. These links are routinely monitored and updated to provide the most current information available.

www.abdopublishing.com

31

Index